SPOTLIGHT ON NATIVE AMERICANS

CHEROKEE

Cassandra Zardes

PowerKiDS
press.

New York

Published in 2016 by The Rosen Publishing Group, Inc.
29 East 21st Street, New York, NY 10010

First Edition

Editor: Karolena Bielecki
Book Design: Kris Everson
Reviewed by: Robert J. Conley, Former Sequoyah Distinguished Professor at Western Carolina University and Director of Native American Studies at Morningside College and Montana State University
Supplemental material reviewed by: Donald A. Grinde, Jr., Professor of Transnational/American Studies at the State University of New York at Buffalo.

Photo Credits: Cover Shutterstock/Waddell Images; pp. 4–5 Dennis Flaherty; p. 7 John Berkey / Getty Images; p. 9 (left) North Wind Picture Archives; p. 9 (right) ...trials and errors; pp. 11, 23 Peter Newark's American Pictures; pp. 12–13 MPI / stringer; pp. 14, 16 (foreground), 19 (right), 24, 27 Native Stock; pp. 15–16 (background) Marilyn Angel Wynn; pp. 19 (left), 21 Corbis; p. 29 (top) Kaldari; p. 29 (bottom) FEMA/Bill Koplitz.

Library of Congress Cataloging-in-Publication Data

Zardes, Cassandra.
    Cherokee / Cassandra Zardes.
        pages cm. — (Spotlight on Native Americans)
Includes bibliographical references and index.
ISBN 978-1-4994-1655-8 (pbk.)
ISBN 978-1-4994-1656-5 (6 pack)
ISBN 978-1-4994-1658-9 (library binding)
1. Cherokee Indians—History—Juvenile literature. 2. Cherokee Indians—Social life and customs—Juvenile literature. I. Title.
E99.C5Z37 2015
796.357'640977866—dc23
                                    2015007808

Manufactured in the United States of America

CPSIA Compliance Information: Batch #WS15PK: For Further Information contact Rosen Publishing, New York, New York at 1-800-237-9932

CONTENTS

CHEROKEE HOMELANDS

CHAPTER 1

The Cherokees are a North American Native people whose homelands in the southern Appalachian Mountains once included parts of present-day Kentucky, West Virginia, Virginia, North Carolina, South Carolina, Georgia, Alabama, and Tennessee. They are by far the largest Native **nation** in the United States, with a total tribal membership close to 275,000 people. Many Cherokees are mixed bloods—part Indian, part non-Indian—due to their long history of **intermarriage** with whites.

Today, about ten thousand Eastern Cherokees live on or near the Qualla Boundary **reservation** in North Carolina, but most Cherokees live in the Cherokee Nation in northeastern Oklahoma. Many thousands also live throughout the United States and in Canada.

It's not known exactly how long Cherokees have been in North America, but by A.D. 1500, they had settled in the Appalachian Mountains. Cherokee origin stories tell of a time when water covered the earth. Land was formed when a water beetle dove deep into the ocean and scooped up mud, bringing it to the surface to make the earth.

The name Cherokee (or Tsa-la-gi) is thought to be a Choctaw word meaning "cave people." The Cherokees' name for themselves is Ani-yun-wiya, meaning the "real people" or "original people."

Home of Cherokees for centuries, the southern Appalachian Mountains in North Carolina are a place of great natural beauty. Today, the Great Smoky Mountains National Park is located near the reservation of the Eastern Band Cherokee Indians.

EUROPEAN ARRIVAL
CHAPTER 2

Before Europeans came to North America, Cherokees were farmers living in villages in Appalachian Mountain valleys. They harvested corn, beans, and squash and gathered nuts, berries, wild onions, and other food in the forest. Hunting provided meat.

By the early 1600s, the English had established colonies along the Atlantic coast. Settlers soon began taking over Cherokee land in Virginia, forcing some villages to relocate farther inland. By the 1670s, Cherokees were trading with the English, exchanging deerskins and animal furs for metal pots, knives, axes, and other useful tools. Before long, they began trading for guns, which they soon became dependent upon.

By 1729, about twenty thousand Cherokees lived in about sixty-four towns. The Cherokees were not able to avoid the wars that Europeans fought with one another in North America, and European armies sometimes burned Indian villages during their own battles.

As the United States became independent from England in 1783, the country's desire for land grew. Settlers flocked into Cherokee country, including present-day Georgia. When the new nation acquired land west of the Mississippi River in the Louisiana Purchase in 1803, President Thomas Jefferson decided that all the eastern Indian nations must give up their land and move west.

In the 1560s, Spanish explorer Juan Pardo traveled through present-day North and South Carolina. This painting depicts his meeting with local villagers from the Cherokee and Creek tribes.

HOLDING ON
CHAPTER 3

The Cherokees realized they could lose their ancient homeland and tried to avoid removal by embracing many white practices, hoping the whites would then consider them as equals. They adopted a written **constitution** and laws, forming a government modeled on that of the United States. They changed the way they dressed and began looking like the white settlers. They also invited **missionaries** into their nation, who started schools and churches.

In 1821, Sequoyah, the son of a Cherokee mother and Virginia fur trader father, invented the Cherokee syllabary. It is a way of writing the Cherokee language that can be learned quickly and easily. The Cherokees soon adopted this system. They began publishing their own newspaper, the *Cherokee Phoenix,* in both English and Cherokee.

Nothing the Cherokees did, however, satisfied the people of Georgia, who wanted Indian land. In 1828, General Andrew Jackson was elected president, promising to remove the Indians from the South.

(*Left*) This painting shows the late 1820s "Southern Gold Rush" on Cherokee land in present-day Georgia. (*Right*) Sequoyah invented the Cherokee syllabary, or writing system. It is still used by modern Cherokees.

In 1829, gold was discovered in the southern part of the Cherokee Nation, and a wild gold rush started. Miners stole the Cherokee gold and demanded the Indians give up their land.

THE TRAIL OF TEARS
CHAPTER 4

Cherokee removal came suddenly. In 1838, General Winfield Scott invaded Cherokee country with seven thousand U.S. Army soldiers and Georgia volunteers. They swept through the countryside, rounding up Cherokee families by the thousands and herding them into prison camps. Hundreds of Cherokees died there from disease.

During the winter of 1838 to 1839, the U.S. Army divided the Cherokees into thirteen groups of about one thousand each and started them west. Many had to walk barefoot on the frozen ground, without enough food and with only one blanket per person for shelter from the cold. The Cherokees traveled about 800 miles (1,300 kilometers) to present-day northeastern Oklahoma, leaving their dead along the way. Their terrible journey became known as the Trail of Tears.

The removal killed about four thousand Cherokees, but many more died of illness after arriving in the West. The Cherokee removal is considered one of the cruelest episodes in U.S. history.

U.S. Army General Winfield Scott was in charge of the Cherokee removal. He became a war hero during the Mexican-American War of 1846 to 1848.

When the great majority of Cherokees were removed in the 1830s, several hundred tribal members in North Carolina claimed they lived outside the Cherokee Nation on land **ceded** to the United States in earlier **treaties**. Though their legal status was greatly in doubt, the U.S. Army did not attempt to remove them.

THE CIVIL WAR
CHAPTER 5

The U.S. government had promised in treaties to protect the Cherokees, but when the **Civil War** broke out in 1861, the government withdrew all its troops in their lands, leaving the Indians helpless. Many had to flee from their homes as armies from both sides swept through their land, stealing all their food and animals and burning almost all the buildings. About one-fourth of the Cherokee people died during the war, mostly from starvation and disease in **refugee** camps.

Cherokees fought on both sides during the war, but the victorious North treated all Cherokees as defeated enemies at the war's end, forcing them to sign a harsh treaty in 1866. The treaty required them to give up land, allow a railroad to build in their nation, and put them under U.S. laws. After the war, whites swarmed onto the Cherokee Nation until they outnumbered the Indians and began demanding their land.

The U.S. Congress began forcing the Cherokees off their land in the late nineteenth century. In 1893, a land run opened on Cherokee land; whites raced one another to stake a claim to a farm.

TRADITIONAL CHEROKEE LIFESTYLE

CHAPTER 6

The traditional Cherokee lifestyle was based on farming; hunting and fishing also provided food. Everyone helped with the town farm plots, and the resulting crops belonged to all. Each family also

Traditional food is an important part of many Cherokee gatherings. Here, the feast includes pig back fat, mustard greens, chestnut bread, and butternut squash.

worked its own fields. Those farms, as well as the family houses, belonged to the women.

The Cherokees grew mainly corn, beans, and squash, as well as many other crops, such as melons and tobacco. They also raised turkeys and hunted them in the wild. After Europeans introduced hogs, cattle, chickens, and horses, Cherokees soon reared them in large numbers.

Experts at harvesting natural resources, Cherokees gathered large crops of pecans and other nuts in the fall, wild onions in the spring, and the blackberries that grew thickly on the hillsides in the summer. Deer, elk, bears, mountain lions, and wolves filled their forests, while herds of buffalo grazed on the famous "blue grass" prairies of their hunting grounds.

European trade goods brought great changes. To have deer hides and animal furs to trade, the Cherokee had to hunt as they never had before—for money. Soon prey became scarce. Hunters couldn't gather enough hides and furs for trade. Before long, the Cherokees had little to trade except their land.

LIFE AT HOME

CHAPTER 7

Cherokee children spent most of their time playing, often with a blowgun made by an older relative from a long piece of cane. Spending many hours hunting squirrels and rabbits in the woods near the village, they learned to shoot darts through the blowgun. When the children were older, they received a bow and arrows and learned to hunt larger game, such as deer. By the time they were teenagers, most young Cherokees were expert hunters.

Generally, women took care of the home, cooked, made clothing, and tended the agricultural fields, while men hunted, made weapons, and fought enemies in times of war. Women could also become warriors, however. Most women did not choose to do so, but some who did became famous, earning the respected name "War Woman."

In a reconstructed Cherokee village at the Cherokee **Heritage** Center in the Cherokee Nation near Tahlequah, a woman is showing how to grind corn into cornmeal.

STORIES AND GAMES

CHAPTER 8

Stories are an important part of Cherokee traditional life, teaching children about their history, traditions, **culture**, and the morals of the Cherokee belief system. According to one traditional story, long ago, the animals held a council to discuss a problem: the people were killing too many animals without showing proper respect for the lives they were taking. Each animal created an illness that would punish the people.

When the plants heard what the animals were doing, they felt sorry for the people, and each plant created a cure for an illness. The story explains how the Cherokees had to learn to show respect for the lives of animals they took and to live in harmony with nature.

Games have also formed a vital part of Cherokee traditional life. Stickball games, similar to the game of lacrosse, were by far the most important. All other activities came to a standstill for a stickball match. **Medicine men** for both sides were employed to make charms that might bring victory in the game.

Frequently, the people bet everything valuable that they possessed on the game. Today, stickball is often played both as a game and as an important part of rituals at ceremonial grounds.

(Left) Today, many Cherokees still prefer to seek the knowledge that medicine men have learned from many centuries of traditional Cherokee medical practice. *(Right)* Stickball remains important to all the southeastern Indian tribes and to many other tribes in North America.

LIVING IN HARMONY

CHAPTER 9

In Cherokee traditional culture, the world was described as being like a giant bowl turned upside down on a saucer, forming a big dome. The earth is underneath the dome, floating on water. The sky fills the dome all the way to the underside of the bowl, which is called the Sky Vault. The Sun travels across the sky each day just beneath the Sky Vault, which is made of rock. At the end of its journey, it slips underneath the Sky Vault to return to its starting point and cross the sky again the next day.

On top of the Sky Vault is another earth-like world. The souls of departed Cherokees live there, along with spirit beings.

An underworld exists underneath the earth. It is just the opposite of life on Earth. When it is daytime on the earth, it is nighttime there. When it is summer on the earth, it is winter there. It is home to many powerful, dangerous spirit forces.

These worlds represent extremes. Traditional Cherokees believe that they live their lives between those two extremes, constantly trying to maintain harmony between the two. Most Cherokee rituals are intended to help maintain that balance.

This mask is used for a traditional Cherokee dance called the Booger Dance. Dances have always been important community activities for Cherokees. They are a time of feasting and visiting.

ART AND LITERATURE
CHAPTER 10

The Cherokees have produced many scholars, writers, **playwrights**, poets, actors, and artists. Some world-famous people, such as Oklahoma humorist Will Rogers (1879–1935), had Cherokee blood.

Lynn Riggs (1899–1954) wrote stories, poems, and 21 plays. One of his plays, called *Green Grow the Lilacs*, was later converted into a musical by Richard Rodgers and Oscar Hammerstein. This became one of the most famous Broadway musicals of all time—*Oklahoma!*

Poet Geary Hobson (1941–), author of *Deer Hunting and Other Poems*, is a professor of English at the University of Oklahoma. He edited one of the most important collections of American Indian literature, *The Remembered Earth*, which was published in 1981.

Rennard Strickland (1940–) has become one of the foremost scholars on Indian law. Strickland has written and edited more than 35 books.

An acclaimed author of children's books about Cherokee life, storyteller Gayle Ross (1951–) has entertained thousands of people with traditional tales.

Entertainer and humorist Will Rogers became one of the best-known Cherokees in the world. He is shown here at his first vaudeville appearance in New York City in 1905.

Novelist Robert J. Conley (1940–2014) brought the oldest Cherokee stories about their history to life in his Real People series. He received the Cherokee Medal of Honor from the Cherokee Honor Society and entered the Oklahoma Professional Writers Hall of Fame. Conley wrote more than eighty books.

EASTERN AND WESTERN CHEROKEES

CHAPTER 11

In the mid-nineteenth century, William Thomas, a white man raised by Eastern Cherokees, bought land for them at the edge of the mountains, property that later became known as the Qualla Boundary. After the Civil War, others joined this reservation in North Carolina.

Eastern Cherokee women compete in a blowgun contest. With practice, the blowgun can be used with great accuracy.

During the twentieth century, tourism became the most important part of the Eastern Cherokees' **economy**. They have built a **casino**, and millions of tourists visit the reservation each year. Parts of the casino profits are used to protect the **environment**, preserve Cherokee heritage, and improve health care, education, and housing.

Today, two Cherokee tribes live within the boundaries of the Cherokee Nation in the West—the United Keetoowah Band of Cherokee Indians, Oklahoma, and the Cherokee Nation. The Keetoowah Band has ten thousand members.

Both these tribes have their tribal headquarters in Tahlequah, Oklahoma. The Cherokee Nation, with over 240,000 members, is not only the largest Cherokee tribe but also the largest Indian nation in the United States by far. It was reorganized in the 1970s. The Cherokee Nation gained federal recognition under a new constitution when the U.S. government gave up its 1907 claim that Indian tribes in Oklahoma had been abolished when that territory became a state.

THE CHEROKEE NATION TODAY

CHAPTER 12

As the U.S. government changed its policy toward Native American governments and upheld laws to allow them to govern themselves, the Cherokee Nation became a leader among Indian tribes. It now manages many tribal programs, ranging from educational programs for Cherokee children to housing programs, which were once run by the U.S. government. This has helped make the Cherokee Nation a large employer in the region, a multimillion-dollar enterprise with a great impact on the local economy.

Today, Cherokee Nation children in northeastern Oklahoma again have an opportunity to learn from Cherokee teachers. Many state public schools in the Nation have Cherokee cultural programs funded by the U.S. government, and many also have Head Start programs, which offer early learning opportunities for preschoolers. The Cherokee Nation now operates Sequoyah High School, which used to be a boarding

Shown here is the Cherokee Nation headquarters building near Tahlequah. The Cherokee Nation tribal complex has many buildings, including a restaurant and gift shop.

school run by the U.S. government, in Tahlequah.

Many young Cherokees stay at home to go to college. Northeastern Oklahoma State University, in Tahlequah, has the highest enrollment of Indian college students of any university in the United States, more than one thousand Indian students each semester. Many of those college students become schoolteachers in the Oklahoma public school system.

PRESERVING THE HERITAGE

CHAPTER 13

Keeping the Cherokee language alive is a priority of the tribes today. Most Native speakers are older people, and numbers are falling. Among the Eastern Cherokees, only around 300 people still speak the language.

Since 2000, the Cherokee tribes have attempted to preserve their language by setting up immersion schools. Children in immersion schools are taught to speak and write in Cherokee. The Cherokee Nation Immersion School in Tahlequah opened in 2003 as a preschool class. Since then it has expanded to include all classes up to sixth grade. In 2009, the Eastern Cherokees opened a similar immersion school, the Kituwah Language Academy, in Cherokee, North Carolina. In 2014, the Cherokee Immersion School in Tahlequah saw its third class of fluent Cherokee speakers graduate.

The Cherokee Heritage Center in Tahlequah and the Museum of the Cherokee Indian in Cherokee, North Carolina, both inform visitors about the history and culture of the Cherokees. In 2010, the Cherokee National Supreme Court Museum opened in Tahlequah. This historic building, the oldest government building in Oklahoma, focuses on the history of Cherokee law, newspapers, and language.

The Cherokee people, both Eastern and Western, are once again governing themselves and are seeking more self-determination for their futures.

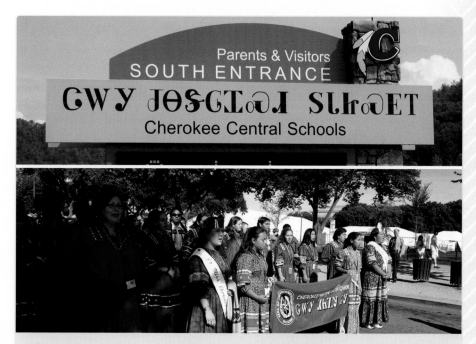

(*Top*) Shown here is a **bilingual** school sign at the entrance to Cherokee Central Schools in Cherokee, North Carolina. (*Bottom*) The Cherokee National Youth Choir takes part in celebrations in Washington, D.C. The choir's members are Cherokee middle- and high-school students.

GLOSSARY

bilingual: Able to speak two languages fluently.

casino: A building where gambling takes place.

ceded: Gave up ownership of something.

Civil War: The war between northern and southern U.S. states that lasted from 1861 to 1865.

constitution: The basic laws and principles of a nation that outline the powers of the government and the rights of the people.

culture: The arts, beliefs, and customs that form a people's way of life.

economy: The way a country produces, divides up, and uses its goods and money.

environment: The natural world.

intermarriage: A term used to describe marriages between members of different groups.

heritage: Traditions, ideas, and objects of value passed down through several generations.

medicine man: A religious leader and healer.

missionary: Someone who tries to teach others their religion.

nation: People who have their own customs, laws, and land separate from other nations or people.

playwright: A person who writes plays.

refugee: A person who is forced to leave his or her home to find safety and protection.

reservation: Land set aside by the U.S. government for specific Native American tribes to live on.

treaty: An agreement among nations or people.

FOR MORE INFORMATION

BOOKS

Machajewski, Sarah. *The Cherokee People*. New York, NY: Gareth Stevens Publishing, 2015.

Schwartz, Heather E. *Forced Removal: Causes and Effects of the Trail of Tears*. North Mankato, MN: Capstone Press, 2015.

Smith-Llera, Danielle. *The Cherokee People: The Past and Present of a Proud Nation*. North Mankato, MN: Capstone Press, 2015.

WEBSITES

Due to the changing nature of Internet links, PowerKids Press has developed an online list of websites related to the subject of this book. This site is updated regularly. Please use this link to access the list: www.powerkidslinks.com/sona/cher

INDEX